"Athens in 3 Day~
Perfect Plan with
to Do in Athens
2017)"

This is a **3 days' guide to Athens**, with a perfect **72 hours plan** that will guide you on the best way to enjoy this amazing city. It includes all tips, maps, costs and information on the destination. Thus, you will feel like you are having your best friend with you, showing you around Athens.

This guide is written by **local experts** and travel **bloggers** who live or visit Athens often. You will get only the best option on where to stay, where to eat, what monuments to see, how to move around Athens. And it will help you to enjoy this vivid city at its best.

This guide includes maps which you can access in their online format, on Google maps. They will enable you to navigate towards them while you are in Athens.

You will find this guide useful if you are a **solo traveler**, or a **couple** or a **group of friends** traveling together to Athens. **Families** traveling with kids to Athens may also find a lot of useful details for planning their trip.

Have fun in **Athens** and thank you for choosing a Guidora guide!

Table of Contents

Athens, the capital of Greece, is one of the oldest cities in the world with a recorded history of at least 3,000 years, consisting the cradle of Western civilization and the birthplace of democracy. Today, the metropolitan area of Athens is the economic, political, industrial and cultural center of Greece.

The city has the 8th position in Europe's largest urban areas and is surrounded by 3 mountains, the **Penteli,** the **Parnitha** Mountain and **Imittos** and 12 hills: **Acropolis, Philopappus, Observatory Hill, Lycabettus, Pnyx,** and **Tourkovounia**.

Land Area: 39 square kilometers
Urban area: 412 square kilometers
Religion: Orthodox Christianity, Catholic Christianity, Islam, Judaism
Currency: Euro (**EUR)**
Euro Equals:
1EUR=1,1USD
1EUR= 83,75INR
1EUR=0,84GBP
1EUR=1,44AUD
1EUR=1,40CAD
1EUR=8,34CNY
1EUR=131,35JPY
1EUR=4,99AED
1EUR=5,09SAR

Climate: Mediterranean climate (hot in the summer and cold in winter).

Do I need a Visa to visit Greece?

In general, vacationing in Greece, which is a European Union Country, for fewer than 3 months, a travel visa is not required. All that is needed is a valid passport. But this depends on your country of origin. Make sure that your passport is valid for at least 6 months after the date of your return from Europe. Members of the EU only need a passport or ID card to travel between countries.

For further information, please check the official site of Ministry of Foreign Affairs in Greece: http://www.mfa.gr/en/visas/visas-for-foreigners-traveling-to-greece/countries-requiring-or-not-requiring-visa.html

Official Language: The Greek Language is the official language. Almost everyone under 40 years in Greece speaks decent English as well.

Time Zone: GMT + 02:00 or UTC + 02:00.

Metric System: Kilograms, centimeters, and Celsius

Electricity: 230Volt and 50 KHz with Type C and Type F sockets.

Currency: The euro (€) is the currency of Greece.

Cost of Living:

-Meal in an inexpensive restaurant: 12 to 15€

- 1.5 liter of Water: 1 €

- Local Transport (one-way ticket): 1.4€

- Cost of a bottle of Beer in a Bar: 5€

- Price of a drink in a Bar: 7€

Double room at inexpensive hotel in Athens: 50 euros/night

Average Internet Speed: 7.3 Mbps (Germany has 12.9 Mbps)

Mobile Telecom Providers: Cosmote, Vodafone, Wind. Cosmote has the best coverage regarding the network.

Cost of SIM Card: You can buy a SIM card for 25 euros which include 2 GB of data.

Dial Code: +30

Health Insurance: If you are coming from Europe bring your EHIC (European health insurance card). More info at http://ec.europa.eu/social/main.jsp?catId=1021&langId=en&intPageId=1739

Vaccinations: No vaccinations are requested to enter the country. You can check the status at https://www.iamat.org/country/greece/risk/routine-immunizations

Important Numbers:

- -Police: 112
- -Ambulance: 112
- -Information of any type like restaurants, hotels, telephone numbers of places, working hours of monuments, etc.: 11880, 11888 (paid service, around 1.5 euro per minute, so be careful).
- -Fire: 199
- -Tourist Police: 171

Lost or Stolen Credit Card:

- American Express: +1 514 285 8165
- Diners Club: +1 514 877 1577
- Discover: +1 801 902 3100
- JCB: +81 3 5778 8379
- Mastercard: +1 636 722 7111
- Visa: +1 303 967 1096

Athens is a city of different aspects. A walk around the famous historic triangle **Plaka**, **Thission**, **Psyri** and the modern luxurious department stores and fancy restaurants near the **Greek Parliament** at **Syntagma Square**, reveals the coexistence of different areas. Here is a map of Athens: http://www.greece-athens.com/maps/

The hotels near **Syntagma Square** seem to be an excellent option for a tourist to live in- both the historic spots and the new aspects of the city are reachable by walk.

Where to Stay in Athens/Our Recommendation: "Central Hotel."

Address: 21, Apollonos street, Plaka, Athens, 10557, Greece
Tel: (0030) 210 3234357 – 9
Website: Click to Read the Reviews on Booking.com and Book It Online
Cost: 80EUR for a double room

The rooms are clean, great value for money and most important the location is perfect, only a few minutes' walk from the main tourist spots such as **Acropolis, Roman Agora, and Greek Parliament.**

How to get to the recommended hotel:

At start take the metro from the Airport Metro Station to **Egaleo** (line 3) and get off at **Syntagma** stop. Go out of the metro, walk to the Syntagma Square with direction to Ermou Street. After 50m turn left onto Nikis street, go straight for 120m and then turn right onto Apollonos Street. Walk about 200m, and you will find the 'Central Hotel' on your left.

09:00

Arrival at **Eleftherios Venizelos International Airport** of Athens, which is 34 km east of the city center.

09: 05

Take the luggage and pass through the passport control- it does not take more than 10 minutes.

09:15

There are various ways to get to the city center. It depends on the amount you can afford. We recommend taking the **metro**. The operating hours are between 6:30 am and midnight.

Where can I find Currency Exchanges and Cash Machines (ATMs)?
In the Arrivals Hall, which is located outside the baggage claim area.

How you can reach the metro
After you have reached the Arrivals' Hall, take the elevator and go to the exit 2 at the Departure Hall. Walk at the rolling walkway for just a couple of minutes, and you will find a rail station. The station is served by both the Athens Metro and the Suburban rail service ('proastiakos'). Take the line 3 of the Metro and stop at '**Syntagma**' stop. The trip from the airport to Syntagma takes about 40 min. You can obtain the metro paper map from the kiosk where you buy the ticket.

Metro map: It is available at https://goo.gl/C9NrKP. You can also check the timetable of the **metro routes** here https://goo.gl/J23Yq6. Before entering the metro station, it is necessary to buy a ticket for 8€ per person (one-way ticket).

Check here all the **tickets' costs** from the airport to the city center:

- One-way ticket for one person: **8.00 €**

- Return ticket for one person: **14.00 €**

- One-way ticket for 2 persons: **14.00 €**

- One-way ticket for 3 persons: **20.00 €**
- One-way half price tickets (students younger than 25, youngsters 6-18, people older than 65+): **4.00 €**
- Children under 6 years: **Free**

Where can I buy a ticket?
You can buy a ticket to the metro station of Athens:
- From the cashier's kiosk in the metro station

- From an automatic dispenser, that sells metro tickets. You can find them near the ticket window, inside the metro station.

Tip: Euro coins and notes are necessary, to pay your fare on the Metro.

Beware of pickpockets
Take any valuables out of your pockets and put them under your clothes (a neck pouch is the best solution). Having a seat is also a good way to reduce the danger from pickpockets who are most active on the crowded trains and metros.

11:00
Accommodate yourself in the hotel and start your day visiting the famous monuments of the city.

The **Acropolis** and the **Parthenon**, in particular, are the most characteristic monuments of the ancient Greek civilization. They continue to stand as a symbol of democracy and the beginning of the Western civilization.
Here you may find the **historical map** of the city:
http://www.greece-athens.com/files/historical_center_map.pdf

How to move in Athens by Metro
Here you can check the costs of all public transport options:
http://www.oasa.gr/content.php?id=tickets&lang=en

Go back to the metro station of Syntagma, take the metro with direction to **Elliniko** and stop at **Acropolis** stop (next stop). Get outside of the metro, walk right at Makrigianni str. And then turn left at Dionisiou Areopagitou str. In a few meters, you will find the entrance of Acropolis.

Acropolis timetable: Everyday 08.00-19.00 Last admission 18.30
Tickets' costs: Full: 12EUR, Reduced: 6EUR
Tickets are available only at the ticket office.
Valid for: Acropolis of Athens, Ancient Agora of Athens, Archaeological Museum of Kerameikos, Hadrian's Library, Kerameikos, Museum of the Ancient Agora, North slope of Acropolis, Olympieio, Roman Agora of Athens, South Slope of Acropolis

Free admission days:
-6 March (in memory of Melina Mercouri)
-5 June (International Environment Day)
-18 April (International Monuments Day)
-18 May (International Museums Day)
-The last weekend of September annually (European Heritage Days)

Reduced admission for:
-Greek citizens and citizens of other Member - States of the European Union aged over 65 years old by showing their ID card or passport
-Students of Higher Education Institutes and equivalent Schools from countries outside the EU by showing their student ID
-The accompanying parents on educational visits to elementary schools.

Free admission for:
-Cultural Card holders
-Journalists with a journalist identity card
-Members of Societies and Associations of Friends of Museums and Archaeological Sites throughout Greece with the demonstration of certified membership card
-Members of the ICOM-ICOMOS
-Persons accompanying blind and disabled
-The escorting teachers of schools and institutions of elementary, middle school, high school, university and graduate level education during their visits
-The official guests of the Greek government, with the approval of the General Director of Antiquities.
-Tourist guides after demonstrating their professional identity of the Ministry of Culture and Tourism.
-University students and students at Technological Educational Institutes or equivalent schools of Member - States of the European Union and students at Schools of Tourist Guides, by showing their student ID
-Young people, under the age of 18, after demonstrating the Identity Card or passport to confirm the age

For further information about Acropolis, check this link: http://www.acropolisofathens.gr/aoa/the-acropolis/monument/#sthash.1pgPDOAU.OQaXwSFD.dpuf

15:00
Visit the Acropolis Museum.

It is on the opposite side of the *Metro Acropolis* station and very close to the Acropolis' entrance. Here you may find all the useful information you may need to visit the museum: http://www.theacropolismuseum.gr/en/content/useful-information You should expect to stay for at least 3 hours in the Acropolis museum, as it is one of the most important things to see while you are in Athens.

19:00
Dinner at the Greek Taverna "Tzitzikas and Mermigas."

Take the metro from the metro station Acropolis towards **Anthoupoli** (this is the red line) and stop at **Syntagma** (which is only one stop away). Go out from the station, pass the Syntagma square, turn left and then right at Mitropoleos str. In about 50m you will find the restaurant.

Greek Taverna: Tzitzikas and Mermigas
Address: 12-14, Mitropoleos str., Syntagma, Athens
Tel.: (0030) 2103247607
Cost: 20EUR per person

Here you may taste some typical Greek dishes. See our guide at the end for more information.

21:00
Enjoy the Greek Nightlife – Have a Drink in "Rock n Roll."

Go to **Kolonaki** district, an upscale residential area northeast of Syntagma with many cafés, boutiques, and galleries. Just 10minutes by walk from the metro station of Syntagma. Go to *Filikis Etairias Square* and have a drink at one of the famous spots of the city:

Visit Bar: *Rock n Roll*
14, Platia Filikis Etairias, Kolonaki, Athens, Tel.: (0030) 210 7220649
Cost: 8-10EUR per person for a drink

01:00 am
Return to the hotel.

Below you can get the maps that correspond to all the activities that we recommend for your first day in Athens. These maps are accessible in Google Maps format so that you can quickly zoom in/out and use them from your tablet or smartphone, when you are in Athens.

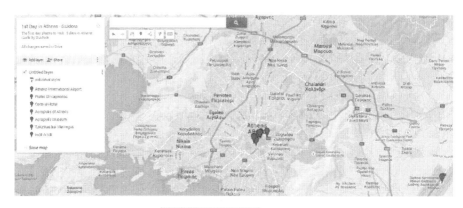

Get this map online at: goo.gl/NxSCi9

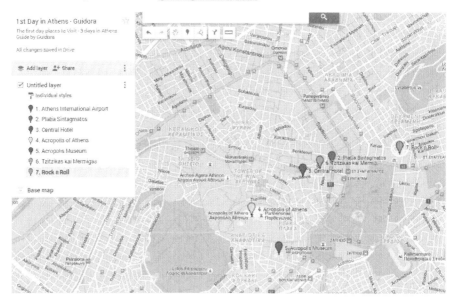

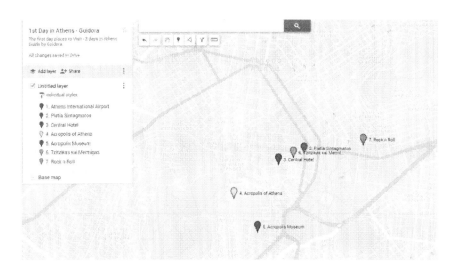

Here is the plan for your second day in Athens.

09:00

Enjoy your breakfast at the hotel and start your day by visiting the National Archaeological Museum.

Go to the Syntagma Metro Station, take the metro to *Anthoupoli* and stop at **Omonoia** Station. Go out from the metro and walk at Eleytheriou Venizelou str.(known as 'Panepistimiou' str.). Turn left at the 1st corner at 28 October str. (known as 'Patision' str.) Walk for about 10 minutes, and you will find the museum on your right.

National Archaeological Museum

Address: 44, Patision str., 10682, Athens
Tel.: 213214 4800
Timetable: Monday: 13:00-20:00pm. Tuesday-Saturday: 08:00-20:00pm. Sunday and Holidays: 08:00-15:00pm.
Website:http://www.namuseum.gr/museum/index-en.html
Ticket price: 7Euros
Note: The National Archaeological Museum is closed: 1st January/ 25th March/ Orthodox Easter Sunday/ 1st May/ 25th-26th December

Reduced admission for Greek citizens and citizens of other Member - States of the European Union aged over 65 years old by showing their ID card or passport.

Free admission for: Cultural Card holders/ Journalists with a journalist identity card/ Members of Societies and Associations of Friends of Museums and Archaeological Sites throughout Greece with the demonstration of certified membership card/ Members of the ICOM-ICOMOS/ Persons accompanying blind and disabled/ The escorting teachers of schools and institutions of elementary, middle school, high school, university and graduate level education during their visits/ The official guests of the Greek government, with the approval of the General Director of Antiquities./ Tourist guides after demonstrating their professional identity of the Ministry of Culture and Tourism./ University students and students at Technological Educational Institutes or equivalent schools of Member - States of the European Union and students at Schools of Tourist Guides, by showing their student ID/ Young people under 18 after showing an ID card

12:30
Visit the Benaki Museum.

The Benaki Museum was founded in 1930 by Antonis Benakis and presents the historical and cultural development of the Greek nation.Go to Omonoia Station and take the metro for Elliniko and stop at Syntagma. Go out and walk at Vassilissis Sofia's str. For about 10 minutes. You will find the museum on your left hand.

Benaki Museum-Main Building

-Address: 1 Koumbari St. & Vas. Sofias Ave.
-Tel.: (0030) 210 367 1000
-Ticket Price: Full admission: €7 Temporary Exhibition: €5
-Reduced admission: Temporary Exhibition: €3, Journalists: €1
-Free admission: Every Thursday (from 15/07/2013 to 15/07/2014) except guided groups and the International Museum Day (May 18th)
-Timetable: Wednesday, Friday: 9:00 - 17:00. Thursday, Saturday: 9.00-24.00.Sunday:9:00-15:00
-Holy Week Timetable (Orthodox Easter)**:** Wednesday: 9:00 - 17:00 /Tuesday: 09.00 - 17.00 (only The Shop)/ Thursday: 9:00 - 24:00 /Friday: 12:00 - 18:00/ Saturday: 9:00 - 15:00
-Closed on Monday, Tuesday and on the following holidays: March 25th, May 1st, August 15th, October 28th, Christmas Day and Boxing Day, New Year's Day, Epiphany, Easter Day, Easter Monday, Clean Monday, Holy Spirit Day.
-The Shop is open during the opening hours of the Museum and on Monday, too.
-The Café - Restaurant is open during the opening hours of the Museum.

15:00

Lunch in the Greek Restaurant "Kuzina."

Now, it is time for you to enjoy the famous Greek dishes in the Greek restaurant "Kuzina."

Greek Restaurant "KUZINA."

Address: 9, Andrianou str., Thissio
Tel.: +30 210 3240133
Cost: 25-30EUR per person
Directions: Go to the metro station of Syntagma, take the metro to Egaleo and stop at Monastiraki. From there take the train to Piraeus and get off at **Thission** (next stop).

17:00

Enjoy a Greek coffee and a great dessert under Acropolis temple at "Chocolat Royal."

Enjoy a coffee and a great dessert with the view of Acropolis. Walk at Asomaton street (next to 'Kuzina' restaurant) and then Apostolou Pavlou street and you will find the café on the right hand. Choose a table at the terrace of the café to enjoy the breathtaking view.

Chocolat Royal

Address: 23, Apostolou Pavlou Str.
Tel: + 30 2103469077
Website: http://www.chocolatroyal.gr/

19:00

Walk at Psiri district and enjoy a 'rakomelo' or ouzo (typical greek drinks) at "Liosporos."

"Liosporos Bar"

Address: 24, Miaouli str., Psiri, Athens
Tel: +30 210 2311841
How to go there: Go out of the café 'Chocolat Royal,' turn left to walk at Apostolou Pavlou str., then turn right and in a few meters you will find the Thission train station. Take the train with direction to

18

Kifissia and stop at **Monastiraki** station. Walk at the opposite site of the train station, near Ermou str. and you will reach Psiri district. This area is full of bars, cafés, theaters, and restaurants.

21:00
Dinner with Live Greek Music at "Stou Korre" Greek Tavern

Stou Korre
Address: 20-22, Agion Anargiron Street, Psiri, Athens
Tel: +30 210-32.15.291
Website: http://www.stoukorre.gr/portal/επικοινωνία

23:00
Return to the hotel.
It is about 25 minutes by walk. Otherwise, take a taxi. It will cost about 5EUR.

2nd Day in Athens - Map

Get this map online at https://goo.gl/xgVKSG

3d Day in Athens

Here is the plan for your third day in Athens.

09:00

Visit the Museum of Cycladic Art.

More than 3.000 objects of Cycladic, Ancient Greek and Cypriot art (dating from the 5th millennium BC to the 6th century AD) are displayed in the galleries of the four floors of the Museum of Cycladic Art. Go to Vassilissis Sofia's str. (near the Syntagma metro station). After 500meters turn left at Neofytou Douka str. and you will reach the museum.

Museum of Cycladic Art

Address: 4, Neofytou Douka street, 10674, Athens
Tel: (0030) 210 7228321-3
Website: http://www.cycladic.gr
Timetable: Monday-Wednesday-Friday-Saturday: 10:00-17:00pm. Thursday: 10:00-20:00pm. Sunday: 11:00-17:00pm.
Note: The museum is closed on Tuesdays and on Public Holidays (1 January, Easter, Easter Monday, Spirit Monday, 1 May, 25 December, 26 December, Shrove Monday, 25 March, 15 August)
Ticket Price: Standard: 7EUR (except for Mondays). Monday's fee: 3,5EUR
Reduced: Seniors over 65: 3,5 EUR/ Students 19-26years old: 3,5 EUR/ Groups of 15 or more: 5 EUR (each)
Free Entrance: Young Persons under 18/ Visitors with disabilities/ Members of the MCS/ Archaeologists and students of art and archaeology/ Members of ICOM-ICOMOS/ Journalists/ Qualified Guides/ Teachers who accompany school classes/ Parents who accompany their kids for the Saturday's program

11:00

Visit the National Garden, Zappeion, the Temple of Olympian Zeus, the Hadrian's Arch and the Panathinaiko Stadium.

Walk at Vassilisis Sofia's Str. at the opposite side of the museum with direction to Syntagma. On your left, close to the Greek parliament, you will find the entrance to the **National Garden**. This was the garden of the palace, created by Queen Amalia and her German gardener Smit in 1839. There you may find many trees, flowers as soon as ducks and a small zoo.

Inside the National Garden, there is **Zappeion**, a building generally used for meetings and ceremonies, both official and private. Near Zappeio and the National Garden, there is the **Hadrian's Arch**, the symbolic gateway between the old city district and the new Roman-built city, erected by Hadrian. The Arch stands in front of the once magnificent **Temple of Olympian Zeus** (the Olympieion).

Behind the Zappeion, the National Garden and the Temple of Olympian Zeus is the **Panathinaiko Stadium**, the stadium that housed the first modern day Olympic Games of 1896.

15:30
Lunch – Try the famous kebab of "Thanasis" Greek Tavern.

Greek Kebab Tavern 'Thanasis.'
Address: 69, Mitropoleos street, Monastiraki, Athens
Walk at Ermou str., the pedestrianized street at the opposite side of the Greek Parliament-Syntagma. The heart of shopping beats here. At the end of Ermou str., on your left hand, there is Monastiraki square. 'Thanasis' kebab is next to the square.

17:00
Taste Greek coffee and traditional sweets under the monument of Acropolis at "Yiasemi"
Walk at the Andrianou str., to reach the Plaka area.

Coffee Shop: "Yiasemi."
Address: 23, Mnisikleous str., 105 55,Plaka, Athens, http://www.yiasemi.gr/

18:30

Taste or buy traditional sweets, such as 'tsoureki' and 'baklava' at one of the best pastry shops in Athens.It is only 10min by walk from Plaka area.

Sweet Shop: "CHATZIS."

Address: 5, Mitropoleos, Syntagma, Athens
Website: http://chatzis.gr/

19:30

Return to the hotel and rest

21:00

Have Dinner at "Stamatopoulos" Greek Tavern

Greek Tavern: "Stamatopoulos"

Address: 26, Lissiou str., Plaka, Athens
Tel: (0030) 210 3228722
Website: http://www.stamatopoulostavern.gr/
The restaurant is only 5 minutes by walk from the hotel. Head west on Apollonos str. towards Ipatias str. After 100m turn left onto Thoukididou str. Then turn right onto Navarhou Nikodimou str. and continue onto Flessa str. At the end of the street you will find the Lissiou str., where is the tavern.

23:00

Enjoy your drink at the square (Platia in Greek) Agias Eirinis-only 10 minutes by walk, at "Tailor Made" bar.
Head northwest on Lissiou toward Erechtheos. Turn right onto Mark Avriliou str. Mark Avriliou str. turns left and becomes Pelopida. Turn right onto Aiolou and after 300m you will see the church of Agia Eirini (Santa Eirini) on your right and a square full of bars.

Bar: Tailor Made

Address: 2, Plateia Agias Eirinis str., Monastiraki, Athens
Tel: (0030) 21300 49645
Website: http://www.tailormade.gr/

01:00
Return to the hotel

You can use Uber or "Taxibeat" in Greece. Taxibeat is an app available for iOS, Android and Windows Phone, which is the equivalent of Uber in Greece and is much more popular than Uber.

You can get this map online at Google Maps format at
https://goo.gl/jh68eA

How to Get From The Hotel to the Airport

Check out from the hotel. Take the metro from Syntagma with direction to the International Airport of Athens 'Eleftherios Venizelos'.

Duration: 40minutes

Ticket costs:

- One-way ticket for one person: **8.00 €**
- Return ticket for one person: **14.00 €**
- One-way ticket for 2 persons: **14.00 €**
- One-way ticket for 3 persons: **20.00 €**
- One-way half price tickets (students younger than 25, youngsters 6-18, people older than 65+): **4.00 €**
- Children under 6 years: **Free**

- Starting charge: 1,19 €
- Daytime charge (tariff 1): 0,68 €/km. The daytime charge applies from 05:00 to 24:00. The taxi meter should be at tariff 1.
- Night-time charge: 1,19 €/km. Night time charge applies from 24:00 to 05:00. The taxi meter should be at tariff 2.
- Extra charge for every luggage heavier than 10 kg: 0,40 €
- Minimum charge for Athens and Thessaloniki: 3,16 €
- Minimum charge for the rest of the country: 3,00 €
- Pick up charge for ports, bus and train terminals: 1,07 €
- Extra charge from/to Thessaloniki airport (includes motorway tolls): 2.80 €
- Pick up charge from/to other airports (includes highway tolls): 2.30 €
- At Christmas and Easter time an extra 1-2 Euro is charged as a present.
- Per hour waiting for charge: 10,85 €/h

The two most popular online/mobile apps for taxis in Athens are **Taxibeat** and **Uber**. There is also **"Taxiplon" app.**

The Absolute 10 Best Day Trips from Athens and Where to Book them Online

Athens is not only a stop-over for the famous Greek islands, or a 2-day short stay to see Acropolis, Plaka, and the Museums. Athens provides you with an excellent opportunity to organize several day trips which may include sea, islands, sailing, history, ancient temples, and amazing scenery. We picked the ten best day trips you can organize from Athens.

#10 Day Trip to Ancient Corinth

The Temple of Apollo God in Corinth - Photo by isawnyu

Corinth used to be the "Monte-Carlo" of the ancient Athens. A vibrant city, 100kms away from Athens, close to the sea, with a lot of commerce, fun, and even famous prostitutes, who were keen to try and indulge with their beauties the wealthy Athenians. The ancient Corinth was built on the top of a hill, and you will need around 1 hour and a half to get there from Athens. It's a nice day trip but not on the top of our list, so don't prioritize it if you don't have many free days in Athens.

Starting from Athens, you will pass through the **Corinth Canal**. This is a Canal opened 100 years ago so that the boats could pass from the Corinthian bay to the Saronic bay. Thanks to this canal, the ancient Corinth was ruling the ancient world of commerce and was considered to be the richest city in the ancient world for quite some time.

Now, you may ask yourself: *"You told us that the Canal of Corinth was opened 100 years ago. How come the ancient Corinthians were making money from it?"*.

Well, the answer is called **"Diolkos."** Diolkos was a paved road that started from the one side of the Corinth Canal and ended to the other end. The workers pulled the ship out from the sea, placed it on big trees and pulled them to the other side of the Canal. This was happening for thousands of years until the canal was excavated and a Seaway was opened. You can still see a part of this ancient road (Diolkos) in the Corinth Canal.

Part of the ancient road (Diolkos) that was used to pull the ships from one side of the Corinth Canal to the other. The Greeks constructed this road around 700 years BC.

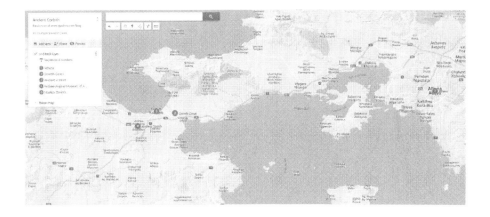

In a day trip to Ancient Corinth, you should spend some time gazing at the **Corinth Canal**, then going to visit the **Temple of Apollo**, then paying a visit to the **Archaeological Museum of Ancient Corinth** and then return to Athens. You could also combine it with spending some time at Xylokastro if you want to enjoy the crystal-clear waters of the Corinthian bay.

The Corinth Canal - Photo by Andrew and Annemarie

The Archaeological Museum of the Ancient Corinth is inside the archaeological area of ancient Corinth. The most important things to see are a marble sphinx, mosaic floors and many coins and everyday objects from the ancient Greece. The entry ticket costs **6 euros**, and it is open from **08:00 to 15:00.** Below you can see a couple of photos with interesting exhibits from the museum.

Corinth costs around **60 euros per person,** and you can book a Half Day Trip to Ancient Corinth at https://goo.gl/aHwDiS.

Guidora's View: We believe that it is overkill to spend a full day for ancient Corinth. Don't do it. Spend only half a day in Ancient Corinth, or combine it with Nafplio (for the romantic walks in this Italian-style city) and Mycenae (for the ancient monuments) or with Xylokastro (for the beach fun).

9 Day Trip to Xylokastro

Kite Surfing in Xylokastro Beach - Photo by Amphithoe

Xylokastro is a beach town on the Corinthian bay, which is 140kms away from Athens and you can reach it in 1 and a half hours with a car. The Xylokastro town does not give you something special as an architecture but what you will enjoy are the small villages built close to Xylokastro (such as **Likoporia, Pitsa, Loutro**). These little villages have many traditional houses, with gardens full of lemon trees, just in front of the Corinthian bay and under some impressive mountains and rocks. In Xylokastro area, you can enjoy several beach sports such as Kite, Windsurfing, SUP, Scuba Diving.

In the middle of Xylokastro, you will find "Pefkias," a forest just in front of the sea. You can just grab a seat at a beach bar under the trees and jump into the clear sea waters whenever you feel like it. There is no entrance fee for Pefkias forest. If you choose to sit on the sunbeds of a beach bar, you will have to pay for the umbrella set (be careful as in some places you may pay up to 15 Euros for two sunbeds and one umbrella).

Pefkias forest on the beach of Xylokastro

Guidora's View: We suggest that you combine a tour to **Ancient Corinth with a visit to Xylokastro**. This is entirely possible if you start your day early. E.g., you can leave from Athens at 08:00, reach the archaeological area of Ancient Corinth at 09:15, spend 3 hours there, then transit to Xylokastro at around 13:00, spend another 5 hours and be back to Athens at around 19:30. Xylokastro is the best area of the Corinthian bay for swimming, so avoid going to other areas such as Kiato, the Modern Corinth, Loutraki, etc. Unfortunately, there is no organized tour that we can recommend to you that goes both to the Ancient Corinth and to Xylokastro. If you feel like spending the evening in Xylokastro, the best hotel to stay is **"Sikeon Resort"** on the beach and almost inside the Pefkias forest. However, it is also the most expensive, so you should expect to pay around 120euros for a double room.

The ancient temple of Athina Afaia *in Aegina Island -* Photo by SteliosKiousis

Aegina is an island in the Saronic Bay, which is **35 minutes** away from Piraeus port of Athens if you take the fast boat. Alternatively, if you get the cheaper and slower boat, it will take you 1 hour and 15 minutes to get from Piraeus port to Aegina island.

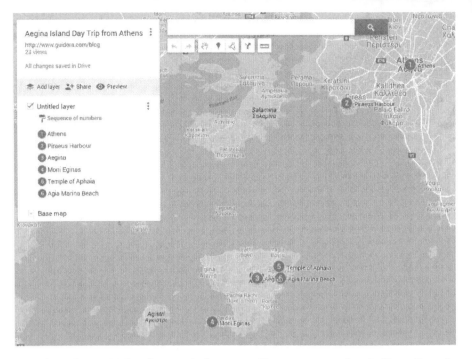

Aegina Day Trip from Athens – *You can get the Online Google Map to Aegina at* https://goo.gl/8QsNWL

Aegina has three thousand years of history and a visit to this place will give you a combination of experiences: Ancient temples, beaches, lovely food and a beautiful main town/village. Some of the top things to do in Aegina are:

- Swim in **Agia Marina beach** or in anyone else that you may find in the coastline on your way there.

- Visit the temple of **Athina Afaiou**

- Have a walk in the beautiful **main village of Aegina**

- Enjoy the Greek food in the taverns and restaurants of the island. Search for **"Nontas", "Skotadis", "Kappos Etsi", "Kavouropetra", "Dromaki", "Babis", or "Argiris".**

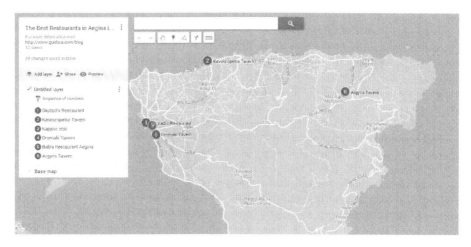

***The Best Restaurants in Aegina. Get it online at
https://goo.gl/73yED8***

Guidora's View: We do recommend you spend a whole day in
Aegina island if you are visiting Athens from May to October when
the weather is nice. The sea water in Aegina is cold until June, and it's
more convenient to swim from July until the middle of September. Of
course, you don't go to Aegina for the beaches. If you are looking for
islands with fantastic beaches, you must go to the Aegean islands or
the Ionian islands. Not to the Saronic islands. So, why bother going to
Aegina? It's close; it has a beautiful town, decent beaches and you will
enjoy a great day, without spending a lot of time to get to the island.

We also recommend that you get a tour to all 3 Saronic islands in one
day - particularly if you don't have so many free days during your visit
to Athens. You can book a tour to Aegina, Hydra and Poros islands at
https://goo.gl/uUoa8G.

Photo by Jaysmark ©

Mycenae was a very powerful city in Athens, especially during 1600 - 1100 BC. At its peak, 30.000 Greeks were living in Mycenae. The King of the Greeks, in the war of Troy, to get the beautiful Helen back to Greece, was Agamemnon, the King of Mycenae.

The whole area of Mycenae is being excavated during the past 120 years, and more and more exhibits come to light.

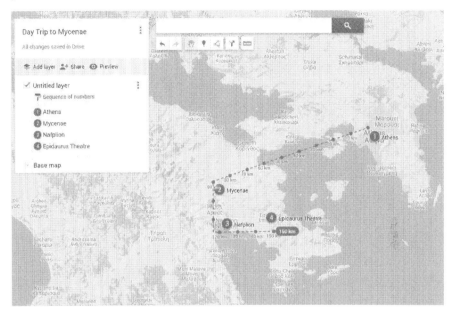

Day Trip to Mycenae – Get it at https://goo.gl/ZyEENv

An excellent company to a book a tour to Mycenae is this one (https://goo.gl/E6f4we), which offers a day trip to Mycenae, Nafplio, and Epidavros with around 70 euros per person.

Guidora's View: Don't spend a full day in Mycenae. It's a nice place but not for more than two hours. You will have to combine it with at least Nafplio to make the trip worthwhile - even better if you can combine it with Nafplio and Epidavros theater (don't go the city of Epidavros, just visit the ancient Epidavros theater).

The ancient Epidavros Theater - Photo by Flickr.Annie Andrews
(cc)

Epidavros was a small city close to Mycenae, and it was the known as the healing center of the ancient world. The healing center was named **"Asklepeion."** Everyone came to Epidavros to get cured, and this has brought a lot of wealth to this little place. Thus, a beautiful theater was constructed on top of a hill, which operates until today. Don't miss the opportunity to grab a ticket for the theater plays that are pretty popular during the summer season, as hoards of locals and tourists come to Epidavros theater to watch them. Epidavros is around one and a half hour away from Athens.

An excellent company to a book a tour with to Nafplio is this one (https://goo.gl/4S7uJk), which offers a day trip to Mycenae, Nafplio, and Epidavros with around 70 euros per person.

Photo by max_ilias ⓒ

Nafplio is a seaport town in Peloponnese, around 1 hour and 15 minutes away from Athens. It was the first capital of the modern Greece. Due to its strategic location, it was conquered by **Ottomans** and by the **Venice** empire. You know that Venice was the richest place on earth for a couple of centuries, so Nafplio has many buildings built with the Venice Architecture norm. It's a romantic place to spend a day, strolling around in its beautiful streets and feeling a little bit like being in Italy.

The Italian-style Streets in Nafplio - Photo by Tilemahos Efthimiadis

A friendly company to a book a tour with to Nafplio is this one (go to https://goo.gl/gYR27y), which offers a day trip to Mycenae, Nafplio, and Epidavros with around 70 euros per person.

#4 Cape Sounio

The Temple of Poseidon in Cape Sounio - Photo by limitsios

Cape Sounio is 70 km away from Athens, and you can reach it in an hour, driving on the seaside road of the Athens Riviera. Sounio is famous for the Temple of Poseidon that resides there. Particularly during the sunset, it offers a fantastic scenery. During the summer period, you can also swim in the beautiful bays that are close to the Cape Sounio or get a sailboat to cruise in its bay.

Cape Sounio also has an interesting mythological story. According to the legend, the ancient King of Athens, named **Aegeus**, has sent his son to fight with the ancient monster, the **Minotaur** in Crete. Aegeus told his son: *"If you return from Crete as a winner you must have the **white** sails on your boat. If you die, please ask the sailors to have the **black** sails up."*

His son went to Crete, fought Minotaur and won. However, he forgot to change the sails to the white color. Aegeus was looking over Cape Sounio for the boat of his son, and when he saw the black sails, he thought that his son was killed. So, he felt from the rock of Cape Sounio into the sea and killed himself. The sea got its name from the King Aegeus and is called until nowadays "Aegean Sea."

#3 Three Days Trip to Hydra, Poros, and Aegina Islands (the three Saronic Islands)

Photo by Tilemahos Efthimiadis ⓒ

The Saronic Bay is the Bay that starts just in front of Athens (Piraeus port). Its most famous islands are Hydra, Poros, and Aegina. If you have a couple of free days, you can combine all three islands on the same tour and enjoy the Greek sea, sun, and food.

If you only have a day to spend, you can book this tour to the Saronic Bay (go to https://goo.gl/XvHaaH). The cost is around 80 euros per person. Another popular tour company you can book with for a Saronic Bay Islands Tour is also this one (https://goo.gl/gs8z4H).

#2 Day trip to Hydra Island

Photo by bwgtheatre ©

Hydra island is the most popular island of the Saronic bay. It is a place where cars are not allowed, and you can only move around the island on foot or by using the traditional donkey-operated vehicles. Hydra was once inhabited by the richest Greeks, mainly ship owners, and it played a very critical role in the liberation of Greeks from the Ottoman Empire, during the Greek Revolution which took place on 1821. In Hydra, you will see many nice buildings, built 60-70 years ago, eat at traditional and elegant restaurants and jump into the sea directly from the rocks, as it doesn't offer any sandy beaches.

Delphi was the ancient oracle of Greece. Every important personality was visiting it to get the "orders and will of the twelve gods". Delphi is built on the top of Mount Parnassos and there is an interesting legend on how this place was chosen. The legend says that God Zeus was looking for the epicenter of the earth to built this center. So, he sent one eagle towards the east and a second one towards the west. The point where the two eagles met each other was this place on the top of Mount Parnassos. And Zeus order to have Delphi built there.

You can book a one day tour to Delphi here (https://goo.gl/w8ZT8F). The cost per person is usually around 70 to 90 euros.

Yes, we know..When you think of Paris, you think of romance..and when thinking of Athens, you are thinking about Acropolis, souvlaki, museums, ancient staff and the islands close to it..Romance does not even make it to the top 5 things people have on top of their mind about Athens..

But! I can assure you that there are some great places in Athens, that could make even Paris get jealous of them..I compiled a list for your reference, and it is highly recommended that if you pay a visit to Athens, you visit at least one of them with your beloved partner.

General Tip: You can make a reservation for free to some of these restaurants through https://www.e-table.gr/en

So, let's get start our romantic journey:

#1: Island Restaurant in Varkiza, Athens Riviera.

Decription: This is a restaurant that always reminds me of being on an island, especially the ones in Cyclades, with the white, paved roads. It's a restaurant built on top of the rock, next to the sea of Athens. It's about 25kms from the center of Athens, so it's not that easy to reach this if you haven't rented a car. The taxi could easily be 25-30 euros to take you there from the center of Athens. The food is nice, even though overpriced and the view is amazing. Late in the evening, there is an open space bar that plays nice music and Island turns into a fancy music club. This is not a place for the budget-seeking food and romance lovers. You should expect to pay at least 60 euros per person for your dinner and another 5 euros for your parking in the area.

Here is a photo from Island Restaurant:

Reservations: Yes, you should reserve a table, especially in the summer period. Don't go here in the winter it's too cold (and usually the restaurant is closed)

Website: http://www.islandclubrestaurant.gr/

#2 Orizontes Lykavitou Restaurant

Description: Lykavitos is the highest hill in the center of Athens. You need a cable car to go there, and once you reach the top you can have the best view of the whole Athens area, all over to the sea. You can also enjoy Acropolis, with its magnificent lights, in the evening and if you are lucky to get a full moon, the evening will have an amazing scenery to start with. The food is very nice, not spectacular but it's a good price for the whole experience you get. You can get a set menu from around 30 euros per person. Please bear in mind that you will have to get a cable car to get to the restaurant and the ticket costs 15 euros for both ways for one person. As a tip, you can mention that you are going to the restaurant (and not just to visit the hill) and if you have a reservation made under your name, the ladies that operate the cable car will double-check it with their list and the price for the ticket will get down from 15 euros per person to 10 euros per person.

Here is a photo from Orizontes Lycabettus Restaurant:

Tip: Ask to be seated outside and on the verge of the restaurant so that you get the best view. Do NOT sit inside the restaurant, as you will most probably miss the experience of the amazing scenery.

Orizontes Lycabettus Menu: You can get it at: http://www.orizonteslycabettus.gr/main-menu/

Website: http://www.orizonteslycabettus.gr

#3 Matsuhisa Restaurant in Athens

This restaurant is located in a fantastic area, in "Asteras Vouliagmenis" beach in Athens and offers amazing views during the evening, towards the Athens Riviera. It serves sushi and Japanese finger food, and it is quite expensive - you should expect to pay at least 70 euros per person for a typical dinner.

Website: http://www.matsuhisaathens.com/

Menu: http://www.matsuhisaathens.com/menus-2/

#4 Varoulko Seaside Restaurant

Varoulko restaurant is owned by probably the most well-known Greek Chef, Mr. Lazarou, who specializes in fish dishes. This gourmet restaurant is in Piraeus and next to the sea. Although it does not offer the same amazing views with the previous 3 restaurants mentioned above, we have this in the list as it is a nice combination of delicious food and scenery. It is also expensive, and you should expect to pay around 60 -80 euros per person for your dinner.

Website: www.varoulko.gr

#5 Dionysos Zonars Restaurant

If you want to enjoy the magnificent view of Acropolis, while eating a great traditional Greek food dinner, you should visit Dionysos restaurant. You should expect to pay more than 50 euros per person for your meal.

Website: http://www.dionysoszonars.gr/

#6 Acropolis Museum Restaurant

This is a budget solution, mainly suitable for lunch. You can visit the Acropolis museum and tell to the ticket office that you only want to visit the restaurant, which is on a balcony that offers an amazing view of Acropolis. It is a budget friendly place where you can have a decent lunch with 20 euros per person, although the "restaurant experience" that it offers cannot be compared to what you get from the previous 5 restaurants. But this is the best solution if you are doing sightseeing in Acropolis and in Plaka/Monastiraki and you still want to enjoy your lunch in a place with great views.

Website: http://www.theacropolismuseum.gr/en/content/cafe-restaurant

That's all from us! We hope you enjoy your romantic lunch or dinner in Athens and drink a glass of Ouzo to our health!

Greece offers amazing food, with local vegetables, cheeses, and meat. Although the menu could be huge and cover every passion you may have, here is a list of the must-try dishes in Greece.

A. Try these amazing Greek Food Starters:

1.Tzatziki (yogurt with cucumber and garlic)

Tzatziki is a Greek sauce that you can try with grilled meats or as a dip with bread. Tzatziki is made of strained yogurt which comes from sheep or goat milk and it is mixed with garlic, salt, cucumbers and olive oil. You may add mint, dill or parsley. Try it with bread, fried potatoes, and grilled meat or grilled fish. And get a mint for your breadth afterward

Melitzanosalata (eggplant salad).

This is made with eggplants, olive oil, garlic and sometimes with Greek cheese (feta cheese) on top, split into pieces. Try it with grilled meat or fried fish.

Ntolmadakia (grape leaves stuffed with rice)

A great starter that you can also find in Turkey. It is made of grape leaves, stuffed with rice and sometimes with mince. Try it with tzatziki (Yes, Tzatziki is like the Coke – you can combine it with almost everything!)

Fried potatoes (Greek french fries)
Make sure you get the fresh Greek french fries. Some restaurants serve pre-fried ones, which are nowhere close to the original ones. Ask before you order.

Greek Salad
This is the most well-known dish of Greece. Amazing salad. Especially in the summer. Cucumber, tomato, Greek feta cheese, onions, pepper and olive oil. Secret tip: Take a piece of bread and make a "dive" as it is called in Greece, in the olive oil, which carries all the flavors of the vegetables.

Souvlaki (sticks with pork meat, grilled)

Try them with Greek French fries, tzatziki, and pita. And a Greek salad.

Paidakia (lamb chops)

These are grilled lamb chops, just with lemon. You know that lamb has a special odor and taste that is quite different from the pork or vein. Some love them, some hate them.

Mousaka

A plate of Turkish origin, with eggplant, bechamel, mince, and sometimes other vegetables. Try one piece. No more.

Pastitsio

Pasta, with mince and bechamel. Fantastic in the summer, together with Greek feta and a Greek salad. Make sure it is freshly cooked and served.

Fish (e.g. ask for Barbounia, Koutsomoures, which are red fish fried)

Stuffed calamari

Grilled Octopus

Spaghetti with Lobster (Astakomakaronada in Greek)

This is one of the most famous dishes during the summer in Greece and especially in the greek islands. There are many ways to cook the lobster when you combine it with Spaghetti. Usually, the cook it with a red sauce from fresh tomatoes and some herbs. It is an expensive dish to try but it worths it!

C. Desserts You Can Try in Greece
Galaktompoureko (milk pie)

Revani

The most famous place for Revani in Greece is a town in northern Greece, called "Veroia". However, you can enjoy this in many places all over Greece. It is like a cake, with extra syrup and a light flavor of orange. Amazing and light!

Greek Halva

Ice-cream (Try kaimaki flavor and add "Vyssino")
Kaimaki flavor is a little bit like vanilla with a twist.

Baklavas Sweet
This sweet comes from Turkey. It is really tasty, and it is quite sweet.

You should also try Greek coffees: Try freddo espresso, freddo cappuccino and greek frappe.

Freddo espresso: A top Invention in Greece, since 2000!
The top invention of the 2000 decade in Greece! Even Italians want to copy this to their own country. You get a hot espresso (double one usually) and you put some sugar in it. Then you place an ice-cube, and you mix it until it cools down. Then you add the ice cubes and you enjoy.

Freddo Cappuccino:

One of the top inventions in Greece! You will not find this easily in other countries, not even in Italy! In Greece, people don't like the hot coffees in the summer. Moreover, Greeks don't like that much the very sweet cold coffees that Starbucks or other similar chains create for the summer.

So, one of the top innovations of the last 15 years in Greece, was the Freddo Cappucino! This is based on the hot espresso coffee and you add some sugar and one ice cube and you mix it. After that, you add the ice cubes. Moreover, you get a milk with full fat and you hit it until it becomes more "foamy" and you add it on top of the coffee you created. The result is the following – usually, people adore it! If you don't like the milk, you can get it just with coffee and without any milk – in that case, it is called "Freddo Espresso".

The best coffee chains in Greece to try that is "Everest", where you can get it in Brazilian or Arabica coffee selection and "Grigoris". Of course, this is a mainstream coffee in Greece and you will find it almost everywhere nowadays.

Greek Frappe:

Italians are great in hot coffees like espresso and cappuccino. Greeks are great in two kinds of coffees: The hot one, which is called "the Turkish coffee – or greek coffee" and the cold ones. The first cold coffee invented in Greece by Nestle, back in the 1980s is the "frappe coffee". This is a really strong coffee that has a special way to prepare. You get some Nestle frappe coffee sliced beans and you mix them with sugar. Then you put some water and you start to shake it, or you mix it with a hand-mixer. Then you add the ice cubes. The result is a cool, tasty coffee, which is called "frappe". It also gets a strong foam on top of it!

It's a strong coffee and you have to drink it slowly, otherwise, you may get an issue with your stomach. Don't drink more than one per day if you are not used to it – otherwise, you will not sleep during the night.

This coffee is not that mainstream anymore in Greece. The young generation snobs it and prefers to drink the Fredo Espresso or Fredo Cappuccino, which are based on the Italian espresso coffee. Actually, we also prefer Freddo Espresso to the Greek Frappe.

What could you ask more? Simply an amazing kitchen, probably one of the best 5 on earth, together with Italian, Mexican, French and Spanish cuisine. Enjoy!

The Best Kept Secret Greek Islands You May Have Never Heard Of

Since you are going to Athens, you may want to spend some days in the Greek islands. As a bonus in our guide to Athens, we offer you the following information on the hipster greek islands that are not that well known to tourists.

Greece boasts an amazing sum of islands (more than 150), some of which are global hits and are world-wide known, such as Creta, Mykonos, Santorini, Corfu, Zakynthos, Rhodes, Naxos, and others.

However, there are many small and hidden gems, unknown to the big touristic masses (20 million tourists per year), that flee to Greece every summer and which are there for you to discover. So, if you feel a little bit more adventurous or you like the backpacking and camping adventure, here is a list of 9 fantastic Greek islands that are almost secret.

1. Koufonissi Island

This is a really small island, in Cyclades Complex, very close to the bigger island of Naxos, from where you can easily get with a boat (or alternatively take a boat from Athens ports). It has become quite trendy to hipster Greeks in the last years, so it is not easy to find a room, especially since it is so small. It has amazing beaches, with white sand and blue waters, a great main town (Chora) with white houses and nice restaurants and tavernas. People go out in the evening to enjoy "Rakomela", which is Raki (a drink like a vodka) with honey. You can also do free camping on a small island which is on the opposite side of Koufonisi island and is called "Kato Koufonisi", which means "Lower Koufonisi" in greek. This island is best enjoyed from couples or group of friends. Prices in the rooms vary from 60Euros per night to 150E per night for a double room.

If you want to visit Koufonisi island, you will have to book your room at least 3 months before, as there are not many options for your stay. Moreover, you will have to pre-book your ferry tickets to go and come back from the island. If you are going to Koufonisi directly from Athens' ports, there is a quick boat that will get you there. Otherwise, you can go to Naxos island and then get a slower boat from Naxos to Koufonisi, as they are close to each other.

You don't need to rent a scooter on this island. You can rent a bike and travel with that to the beaches, which are around 1-2 km away from the main town of Koufonisi (actually, it is the only town on the island and it is a village..)

2. Gaidouronissi Island or Chrisi (South of Creta Island)

An amazing small island with one of the best beaches in Greece, which is situated in the south of Creta. You go there with a small boat that leaves from Crete in the morning and you have come back in the afternoon. Or, you can do free camping there. This is an island with no people living on it – so make sure you prepare accordingly if you plan to stay during the evening.

3. Tzia Island (or Kea island)

This is a great small island, one and half hours away from Lavrio, which is one of the 3 ports of Athens, 60 km away from the Athens town. Tzia is not famous for the beaches but it has a great nature, a fantastic town to visit and is popular with sailors who start from Lavrio port or Rafina port. If you sail, this is probably your first stop. There are many places to visit and enjoy in Tzia island, so you will easily find a room. Stay at Vourkari village, which is in the sea, so that you can enjoy the sailboats that arrive. In the evening, the crews of the boats have drinks at Vourkari, together with ...everybody!

In Tzia island, you can find hotel rooms or apartment rooms starting from 50 Euros per night or even lower at the low season. The high season for Greece is from 20th of July until the end of August, so prices are higher during that period. Plan for a budget of 80E to 100E for a standard room for two persons, during that time.

4. Patmos Island

Patmos may not be that secret anymore. A lot of Italians have discovered the island, especially after some Hollywood stars have selected it for their vacation. This is a sacred island for Greeks, as it has a special religious meaning for the country. Again, the beaches are not the reason to visit the island as the water tends to be quite cold to swim compared to the other greek islands but it has a great town, a great feeling and amazing people that visit it. The rich and famous of Greece and the hipsters, usually pay a visit here, as it has become the place to go, after Mykonos island. It is very far from Athens to go with a boat (around 8 hours), so you should try to get an airplane to a nearby island and get the boat from there.

If you go to Patmos island, don't miss the chance to eat at the "Trehantiri" tavern. This is a family tavern, ran by the captain of "Trehantiri" boat, which brings fresh sea fruits and fishes every day to your dishes. You will be amazed by the quantity you get for the money you pay. Definitely the best value for money tavern on the island of Patmos.

Moreover, go to the Vaya beach and visit the Vaya Cafe, where you should try the famous Chocolate Cake. Simply amazing!

5. Paxoi and Antipaxoi Islands

These are two small islands on the west side of Greece, opposite to Italy. Paxoi is inhabited while Antipaxoi has almost nothing and you get there with a boat from Paxoi island. Both islands and especially Antipaxoi, are famous for the amazing blue-water beaches and the vivid, green nature that cover the islands. Paxoi, however, is a little bit expensive, so plan well ahead. Moreover, it is not easy to find a room due to the small size of the island.

6. Symi Island

What can we say about this paradise island? Probably one of the most beautiful islands in Greece. It has an amazing town built in front of the sea and when you see it for the first time as the boat arrives, you will feel so amazed that you will want to start ..crying from joy! Symi is well-known for its tavernas and food, especially the shrimps, which have a well-known brand name in Greece – make sure that you try them! Again, it is very far from Athens and it doesn't have an airport, so you should fly to a nearby island and get the boat to it.

7. Elafonisos Island

This is a small island in the south of Peloponnese in Greece. It is famous for each beach, which is called "Simos", after the name of the person who has a taverna in front of it. Pretty small, without a lot of things to do. It's just the perfect place to go if you want to relax and enjoy a Hawaii-like beach in Europe.

8. Kithira Island

Kithira is also in the south of Peloponnese and opposite from Elafonisos. It is a big island with amazing nature, great food to try and a fantastic main town built on the top of a hill, into a castle. To go there you either fly from Athens, or you get a boat from Athens, or you drive 4 hours to the south of Peloponnese from Athens and then you get a 1-hour boat to Kithira. The best option is to fly.

9. Folegandros Island

Folegandros is a volcanic island, opposite from the world-famous Santorini island. So, Santorini catches all the glory. Still, Folegandros is much less touristic but offers amazing views and a great town (Chora). The beaches are strange. With black volcanic stones and crystal clear (although cold) waters. You can add Folegandros to your schedule if you plan to visit Santorini. It's far from Athens, so get an airplane to Santorini and a boat from there to Folegandros.

Help with Planning your Visits to the Greek Islands from Athens

Greece is one of the favorite summer destinations and more than 20 million tourists vote for that every year. However, if you plan to travel without a group, you may find yourself confused with trying to book boat tickets, airplane tickets to islands, museum tickets etc.

Here are some links to useful resources to help you plan your trip to Greece:

1. Which are the 3 Ports of Athens, to take a boat to the Greek islands?

Greece has many ports and for many islands, you will find boats starting from different ports. For example, if you are going to the islands of the Cyclades, e.g. Mykonos, Santorini, Paros, Naxos, you can travel towards there from one of the two ports of Athens: Piraeus port or Rafina port. Actually, Athens has a third one, which is situated in Lavrio town, 60km away from Athens, which is pretty close to a couple of Cyclades islands, such as Tzia and Kythnos island.

Below you can see the 3 ports of Athens: Piraeus, Rafina, and Lavrio. Piraeus port is in the closest to Athens city. Rafina is about 30 km outside of Athens and Lavrio is around 60km away from Athens town.

As a general rule: If you are going to any of the islands of Aegina, Agistri, Hydra, Poros, you can only get boats from Piraeus port. If you are going to the islands of Tzia (Kea) or Kythnos, you can get a boat from Lavrio port. For all the other islands (Mykonos, Paros, Naxos, Andros, Santorini, Milos, Amorgos, Koufonisia, Donousa, Shoinousa, etc), you can choose to leave either from Piraeus or from Rafina port. Rafina is closer to many islands of Cyclades, compared to Piraeus port, as you can see from the map, but you will have to travel outside of Athens to get the boat.

2. What are the Types of Boats you Can take to the Greek Islands?

Basically, there are two types of boats you can take to get to any greek islands: The slow ones and the fast ones. E.g., you will see that if you want to go to Mykonos and you want to start from Rafina port, there is a boat that takes 4 hours to get to Mykonos and another one that takes 2 hours to get there. The second type is obviously much more expensive.

Moreover, if you are visiting Greece with a car, keep in mind that not all boats accept cars. Some of them do and some of them don't.

The fast boats are branded usually by Greek Telcos such as Cosmote and Vodafone. E.g. the following one is a fast boat:

Or this one is a fast boat too, but it doesn't accept cars or motorbikes:

The following is a slower boat (even though it says FastFerries!):

3. Where can you Book your Boat Ticket to a Greek island online?

There are a couple of Greek websites that you can use to book online your boat ticket to a Greek island. If you are planning to travel in July and August, please pre-book as soon as possible. Demand is very high and you may end up looking for tickets if you don't plan early.

A website you could use is http://www.viva.gr. Just go to http://travel.viva.gr/en/ferries, input the port you want to leave from (Piraeus, Rafina or Lavrio) and your destination and you will get all the options.

E.g., in the following example you can view the options to travel to Mykonos from Rafina port. You can see how some boats accept cars/motorbikes while some others don't. You can also see that some boats are faster than others.

Also, keep in mind, that if you want to travel between islands, there are some local companies that offer the transportation but you cannot book it online.

4. Get an Airplane to the Greek Islands

If you don't want to use a boat for your transfer to a Greek island, then you may consider getting an airplane to travel to some of them. Many islands have airports but not all of them. The companies that are flying from different areas of Greece to the greek islands are:

– Aegean Airlines: http://en.aegeanair.com/

– Olympic Airlines (actually it is the same company with Aegean airlines, due to a merge that took place): https://www.olympicair.com/

– Ryanair: http://www.ryanair.com

– Minoan Air: http://www.minoanair.com/

– SkyExpress: http://www.skyexpress.gr/en-us/home.aspx

– Ellinair: http://en.ellinair.com/

Out of these, Aegean and Olympic airlines are considered the most respected brands in Greece.

To book an airline ticket to a Greek island, you could use http://www.viva.gr, or http://gr.skyscanner.com/, or book directly from the website of the airline company.

The Greek islands and towns with airports are the following (from Wikipedia):

5. List of Embassies in Greece

Greece hosts embassies from most countries on earth. For detailed addresses and phone contact, you can view this web page.

6. List of Banks in Greece

If you need to withdraw cash from ATMs, Greece has a huge network of ATMs in every place and island. Banks are either Greek ones or branches of international ones. You will not have an issue, no matter which one you use.

6.1 The Greek banks are:

- Alpha Bank:

- Attica Bank

- Eurobank Ergasias

- National Bank of Greece

- Piraeus Bank

The Greek branches of international banks are (source Wikipedia):

6.2 Greek branches of international banks

Bank of America, Bank of Cyprus, Bank Saderat Iran, BNP Paribas Securities Services, Citibank International (now it is bought from Alpha bank in Greece), Credit Suisse Luxembourg, Deutsche Bank, FCE Bank (de), FGA Bank, Fimbank, HSBC Bank, HSH Nordbank,

KEDR Open Joint-Stock Company Commercial Bank, T.C. Ziraat Bankasi, The Royal Bank of Scotland, UniCredit Bank, Unión de Créditos Inmobiliarios (es) (web)

7. Greek Mobile Operators

Greece has 3 mobile operators that use the GSM system. Vodafone, Cosmote, and Wind. You can buy a greek mobile card with prepaid internet and phone credits when you arrive in Greece. Otherwise, you can, of course, use your own and pay the roaming charges. You can find information on the roaming charges at the telcos websites, eg here (https://goo.gl/tgQUAG).

WIND offers 3GB / 30 days for 30Euro with a USB stick and 15 Euro without a USB stick Wind Broadband (https://goo.gl/Sa5GYx)

Vodafone offers 150MB for 30 days for 7 Euros and is charging 1Euro per day after the 150MB are used up. Vodafone Broadband (https://goo.gl/AChmKM)

Cosmote offers 5GB for 30 days for 40 Euros and 1GB per day for 5Euros. COSMOTE Broadband (https://goo.gl/XF5UBh)

8. Find a Doctor in Greece

We wish that you never have to use this service but just in case, if you need to get a doctor in Greece you can do one of the following:

a. Visit a greek site such as http://www.doctoranytime.gr/ (use Google translate)

b. Call one of the information telephone numbers, such as 11880 or 11888. You pay per minute but you can ask any information you want in English and you will get your reply very easy.

Moreover, every island in Greece has a pharmacy store but they are not open all the time.

9. Book a Greek Museum Ticket?

Greek museums do not offer e-tickets currently, so you cannot pre-book them. The lines are not that big usually, so you can buy them on the spot. Just make sure that you check the visiting hours beforehand.

If you are staying in Athens during the summer and you don't want to visit the islands, but you would like to spend a great day on the beach, we recommend that you go to the best beach in Athens, the Astir Beach. This is a guide to help you save money when going to Astir beach and to give you all the information on how to enjoy this beach at its best.

Astir Beach, or Asteras Vouliagmeni Beach, as it is called in Greece, is the best beach that Athens has to offer to locals and visitors. This is a review and a guide to help you enjoy Astir beach at its best while helping you to save up to 75% of the cost to enter this amazing place.

The History of Astir Vouliagmenis Area

We know you love history. So, what is the history behind the whole area of Astir Vouliagmenis?

Astir Vouliagmenis is a living legend of the modern cosmopolitan Greece. Since 1959, the famous hotel in this area, Astir Vouliagmenis Hotel, looks proudly from the top of the hill to the bay of Vouliagmeni. Its name is connected to hosting some of the most important figures in business, politics and the star-world, either from Greece or other countries. Astir Vouliagmenis, actually, belong to the National Bank of Greece and the Greek state, which is looking for a way to sell it to venture funds as part of the privatization efforts that run in the country.

Inside the beach of Astir, there are ruins of a very important ancient temple, the temple of Apollonas Zostiras, which was built in the 6th-century b.c.

According to the legend, the kids of the Vouliagmenis orphanage were playing on the beach and while they were digging they found, during 1924, this temple, which is positioned in a strategic place to control the bay area.

In 1961, the first bungalows started to operate in Asteras and in 1966 the first water ski school in Athens was inaugurated here. Soon after, the beach of Astir was the meeting point of all famous greeks and Athens visitors. In 1969, the Arion hotel was inaugurated and two more hotels were built, the Nafsika hotel in 1979 and the Aphrodite hotel in 1984 – which is not operating anymore.

Aristotle Onassis was one of the most fanatic visitors of Astir, together with Frank Sinatra, Marlon Brando, Paul Newman, Joan Collins and other celebrities of that time.

1. How to Get to Astir Beach: Car, Bus or Taxi

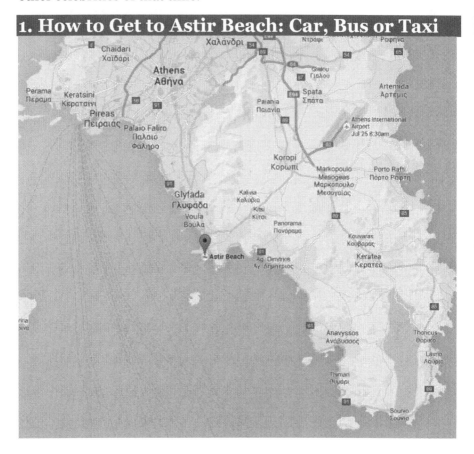

Astir Beach Location

The Astir beach is located in the south suburbs of Athens, in the area that is called "Vouliagmeni". Astir in Greek means "Star Shape" and if you have a closer look at the map you will see that this whole area looks like a half star.

Photo: Astir Beach Area

In this area, there are different things you can find with the name "Astir". The main hotel that exists in this area is called "Astir Vouliagmenis Hotel" and it has also its own private beach.

Additionally, there are two different beaches with the name Astir Beach, one opposite to the other. The first one is a private beach where you pay an entrance to enter and the second one is a public beach, where it is free to swim.

We are now presenting information regarding the private beach of Astir.

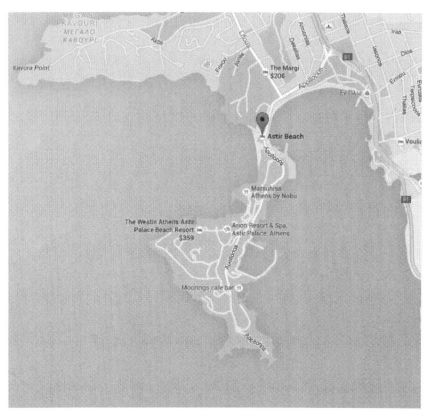

Photo: Astir Beach – A Closer Look

Here is a clearer explanation of the beaches that you can find in this area:

Photo: Astir Beaches

You can get to Astir Beach either via driving your own car or by using public transportation – e.g. a bus from the center of Athens. Unfortunately, there is no underground metro station in Vouliagmeni area.

If you get a taxi from the center of Athens, it is about 22kms, so it would cost you around 30 to 40 euros.

During the weekends, you may encounter traffic from people going to or returning from the beaches in the south of Athens, so it might take you more than an hour to get to Astir Beach if you leave at around 11:00 AM in the morning. Otherwise, it should be around 35 to 40 minutes.

2. Astir Beach Parking and How to Avoid a 40Euro Parking Fine Ticket

There is no parking in Astir Beach, so you have 3 solutions for your parking close to this beach.

The first one is to leave your car on the road, around 500 meters before entering the beach. You will find out that many others leave their car there. It is not legal in most of the places there, so you may get a fine ticket for illegal parking, which costs 40 Euros – and you can get it down to 20 euros if you pay it within the first three days.

The second solution is to drive 20 meters after the entrance of Astir Beach and you will find a parking that belongs to the Sailing Club of Vouliagmeni. It is not allowed to park there but what you can do, is to give 5 Euros to the security guys of the parking and they will drive your car up to the hill and bring it back to you later – it's not an "official" way to park but it saves you from a lot of trouble.

The third solution for finding a parking at Astir beach is to continue driving after the entrance of Astir Beach, go up the hill – around 1km – and park your car in the open spaces next to the road. It will cost you a 10-minute walking down and up the hill – which is especially tedious during the hot summer in Athens.

3. Astir Beach Price/Entrance Fee – How much it costs to enter Astir Beach and How to Save 50%

The Astir beach is a private beach and you have to pay an entrance fee to get inside. The entrance is 15 Euros per person from Monday to Friday and it is 25 Euros on Saturday and Sunday. Kids from 5 to 12 years old pay 8 euros from Monday to Friday and 13 Euros on the weekends. These are the prices for the high seasons, which is from 16th of May until the 15th of September.

There is a trick to save 50% of the ticket fee: If you are a subscriber to Cosmote's mobile network (you can get a Cosmote prepaid mobile card if you are a tourist), you can send an SMS to 19019 and you get 1 ticket for free if you buy 1 ticket, during Monday, Tuesday and Thursday. This way, you pay 15 euros for 2 persons, instead of the 30 euros, you would pay during these days. So, skip going to Astir Beach on the weekends with 25 Euros per person and go on these days that we mentioned, with 7.5 euros per person. Check the website of Cosmote's deal for Astir Beach (https://goo.gl/ktudGK), before you use it, to make sure that no days have changed. The cost of the SMS is 0.5 Euros. The offer is valid for the first 100 persons and for arrival time until 11:00 am according to the rules on the website.

For the price you pay, you get a free set of 2 sunbeds and an umbrella and nothing else. You will have to pay everything else (coffees, water, ice-creams, lunch, etc.), on your own. If you go late to the beach, you will find that all sunbeds are taken, and you will have to wait under a tree, or at a cafeteria, until you get your own. Not the best thing in the world, especially if you consider that you have paid the same price for everyone else.

The sunbeds you are getting for free with your entrance fee

Other Prices Inside Astir Beach:

– A small bottle of water (500ml) costs 1 euros

– A big bottle of water (1lt) costs 2.5 euros

– An ice cream with 2 scoops, costs 4.5 euros

– A cold coffee (freddo espresso as it is called in Greece), costs 4 euros.

4. Astir Beach Times: When to Arrive to Find an Umbrella

The beach is open from 08:00 in the morning until 21:00 in the evening. The best time to go there during the weekends is until 10:00

in the morning. If you arrive later, e.g. at 11:00, you will most probably not find an empty set of sunbeds/umbrella and you will have to wait until one is freed up.

5. Astir Beach Amenities: What you can enjoy during your stay.

The beach offers many amenities that you can use. There is a changing clothes area – separate for women and men. There are shops that sell ice-creams, water, drinks, champagnes, food and you can order them while you are enjoying at your sunbed. There is a "Friday's" restaurant on the beach and you can get a sit and enjoy the dishes of the popular American food chain restaurant.

Moreover, there is a beach volley court for the most athletic among you. And you can try different water sports, such as jet skis, tubes, water ski etc. Holmes place has also a sports area that you can use.

Photo: astir beach volley

Finally, you can enjoy a massage therapy, provided by the Orloff Massage of Astir Beach Hotel, inside the beach.

6. Astir Beach – People: Is it too Posh for you?

The beach has a capacity of around 600-700 umbrella sets, so when it is full, you will find around 1500 people. There are many families from the upper middle class of Athenians visiting this beach. Moreover, as it is a posh beach, you will find famous singers, models, actors, athletes and politicians, enjoying the blue waters of Astir Beach.

You may wonder: *Is it too posh for me?*

The truth is that even though there are many rich people enjoying themselves on this beach, you get a relaxed feeling that will make you feel that you fit in this environment. No, it doesn't feel that posh, don't worry.

7. Astir Beach – Is the beach and the water clean?

Although the beach is very close to the towns of Vouliagmeni, Glyfada it is a really clean beach. It has a blue flag, which is the "certification" for a clean beach. Apart from that, you also see the crystal clear waters when you swim and you get the same feeling that this is a great beach to swim at. The sea is shallow, so it is great for kids too. It is also sandy for at least 70 meters from the shore, so don't expect to find anything interesting for snorkeling.

8. Bonus Tip: How to Make a Reservation for a Sunbed at Astir Beach

Is it possible to make a reservation for the sunbeds at Astir Beach? Yes, just visit this link to make a reservation of your Sunbed at Astir Beach, (http://t.co/cGddnqFrsV).

Relevant information is also available at the phone number: +30 – 2108901619. The price for a sunbed in the reservations area on the weekend is 40 euros for one sunbed and the price during the weekdays is 25 euros per sunbed.

Photo: Sun Bed Reservations Astir Beach

Where to Stay in Athens, if you don't like the Central Hotel Suggestion

If you Plan to Visit Greece, you will most probably stop for 3 or more days in Athens, where you will be wondering what are the top things to do in Athens and what is the best area to stay in Athens to have the best possible experience.

Athens is one of the biggest cities in Europe, with a population of 5 million inhabitants and features many different options for areas to stay at, depending on what you want to do during your stay in Greece's capital. Traffic is also quite heavy and although there is an underground network, it's not that extended, so you should pay attention when choosing your hotel area.

Don't worry! We got you covered. Read below, to get a better understanding of the pros and cons of staying at the different areas of Athens. Information is based on criteria such as Hotel Prices, Proximity to the main attraction areas, Nightlife, Shopping Areas and Safety.

What is The Best Neighborhood to Stay in Athens?

We often get asked, "What is the Best neighborhood to Stay in Athens?". If you want the mainstream and quick answer, we would suggest Plaka, Kolonaki or Psiri.

However, it is not that easy to choose the best area to stay in Athens, as you may want to combine your stay with different experiences, which would require for you to stay somewhere else.

E.g., if you are visiting Athens during the summer, you may want to stay in the Southern Suburbs, so that you are closer to the beach and to the awesome Night Beach Clubs that Athens has to offer.

Moreover, if you are a family and you wonder where to stay in Athens with Kids, you may choose a safer area, which is also more friendly to families such as Kifisia, in the Northern Suburbs.

87

So, allow us to provide you with more information regarding the different areas to stay in Athens, with their advantages and disadvantages.

General Description of the Areas to Stay in Athens.

In general, there are 4 main areas where you can stay in Athens.

The first is the center of Athens, which features the main touristic places and has neighborhoods such as Syntagma, Plaka, Monastiraki, Kolonaki, Omonoia, Alicia, Thiseio, Zografou and others.

The second one is the southern suburbs, which is the beachside of Athens, with neighborhoods such as Vouliagmeni, Alimos, Glyfada, Voula, Elliniko, Faliro and others.

The third area is "Piraeus ", where the biggest port of Greece lies.

The fourth area is the North Suburbs of Athens, with neighborhoods such as Halandri, Marousi, Kifisia.

Below you can see a general map of Athens, featuring these 4 areas. We would not recommend staying in other areas, e.g. on the west or east suburbs, as they tend to be quiet far from the main activities you will most probably pursue while you are in Athens and will not be convenient for your stay.

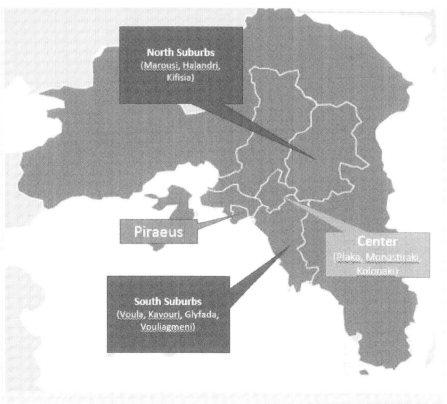

Where to Stay in Athens – Map with the Main Areas

Now that you got a general idea of what the main areas to stay in Athens are, let's have a closer look at each one of them.

1. Staying at the Center of Athens [Museums, Sightseeing, Acropolis, Bars]

Staying at the Center of Athens features quite many different areas, with each one pros and cons. Below, we have prepared a map which features the main areas that you can choose when staying at the center of Athens. The Commercial Area and Plaka, the Acropolis Area, Exarheia, Areos Area, the hill of Lycabettus, Kolonaki area, and Ilisia.

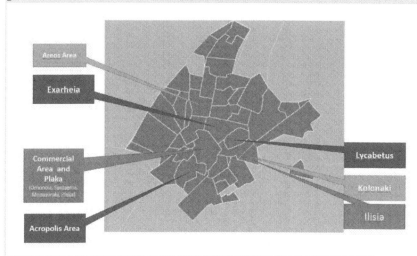

Where to Stay in Athens – Map of the Center of Athens

Let's have an even closer look at these areas:

1a. Staying at the Commercial Area and Plaka [Underground, Bars, Sightseeing, Noisy]

If you choose to stay at the Commercial Area (or commercial triangle as it is called) and the area of Plaka, you will find yourself right in the heart of Athens.

Plaka area is like a small village in the center of Athens. It is below the hill of Acropolis with old, traditional houses and many restaurants, cafes, monuments and things to do.

Plaka is an excellent place to stay, as it is conveniently placed regarding museums, Acropolis, the underground station of Acropolis and the main shopping street of Athens, Ermou street.

The prices are of course higher here and you will not find- easy- value for money hotel rooms. If you are planning for a budget of under 100E per night, you will find yourself in a mediocre type of room, which – on the other side- will be close to everything. This is also a safe area to stay.

Psiri in Athens is also a nice neighborhood to stay if you want to stay near to the center of Athens. Psiri is full of bars and restaurants. Psiri used to be a very poor neighborhood in Athens, which got renovated and is now quite popular to the younger generation of Athenians.

Even thought it was trendy and was visited by the hipsters of Athens a decade ago, it is now being snubbed by them.

The best hotels to stay in Plaka are:

1. The Central Hotel in Plaka: Click to See Rates, Reviews and Book the Central Hotel Online (https://goo.gl/8Nq11T)

2. Electra Palace Hotel in Plaka: Click to See Rates, Reviews and Book Online the Electra Hotel in Plaka (https://goo.gl/BcGsWm)

1b. Staying at Acropolis Area [Quiet, Sightseeing, Difficult Transportation]

Acropolis is on a hill, so the whole Acropolis Area is quiet difficult to walk. Here, you will find hotels in an area that is called "Koukaki" and is 500 meters from Acropolis.

It is a safe area and you might get a hotel with a view of Acropolis and Parthenon. This is not such a convenient place to stay at, not the same with staying in Plaka, as you will have to walk a lot (and usually uphill and downhill), to get to the other side of the hill, where all the action takes place.

The best hotels to stay in the Acropolis area are:

1. The AthensWas Hotel: Click to See Ratings, Reviews and Book Online the AthensWasHotel (https://goo.gl/r2wNd9)

2. Hotel Grande Bretagne: Click to See Ratings, Reviews and Book Online the Hotel Grande Bretagne (https://goo.gl/kB8H8w)

Available rooms | Facilities | House rules | The fine print | See all verified reviews

Superb 9/10
Score from 412 reviews

being on the butler floor and having a seperate reception area to avoid the crowds -

🧑 Sharlene, ▥ United Kingdom

1c. Staying at Exarheia [Hipster, Noisy, Not That Safe, Bars]

Graffiti at Exarheia Street

Exarheia area is very close to the center of Athens. This is the most alternative area of Athens. With a good and a bad sense. In Exarheia you will find the most alternative bars, restaurants, and people.

On the other side, this is the most "revolutionary" part of Athens. Protests start from Exarheia and you may find police giving fights with people belonging to the anarchist groups. It's not easy to judge Exarheia. It has its own character. You either love it or hate it.

Exarheia is not the safest area of Athens to stay at. If you are young and wild you may want to choose it for its own feeling and to get a better sense of Athens. If you are a more conservative traveler, stay away from it.

1d.Staying at Lycabettus [Nice Views, Not convenient for Transport]

Lycabettus is a hill. The second hill of the center of Athens, which is on the opposite of Acropolis' hill. It is very close to the posh area of Kolonaki. As it is on a hill, it offers a fantastic view of Athens and it has some really nice hotels, such as St George Lycabettus, which you will certainly enjoy.

It is also a safe area to stay at. On the downside, you will still have to walk a lot (and uphill/downhill), it is not that close to the underground stations, so we would not recommend staying at this area.

The best hotel to stay in Lycabettus is the Hotel St George Lycabettus (https://goo.gl/pynfNj)

1e.Staying at Kolonaki [Posh, Central, Shopping, Bars, Cafes, No Sightseeing]

Kolonaki is the most expensive area of Athens. It is the main shopping center of Athens, with the most expensive streets, shops, restaurants, and bars.

Although Greece is in a crisis since 2010 and Kolonaki has lost some of its glam, especially visible in the first decade of 2000, it still remains the "VIP" area of Athens. Kolonaki is an old area, so you will not find new hotels or new apartments to stay at.

Kolonaki is a safe area to stay. It is 2kms away from Acropolis, so a 10E Taxi drive to there. The good thing about staying at Kolonaki is that during the evening you will find many bars and restaurants open and usually full of people. Moreover, it features many great shops from top brands, including Louis Vuitton, Armani, Prada, Boss etc. You get the idea.

Kolonaki doesn't have any important museums or monuments to see. Still, it is a safe choice when choosing an area to stay at, if you want to explore the center of Athens and get some fun in the evening. St George Lycabettus is the best hotel in the Kolonaki area. You will not find many hotels to stay here. It is easier to find places from Airbnb (apartments). Please bear in mind that most buildings are very old here, so the apartments might be over 40-50 years old.

1f.Staying at Ilisia [Student Area, Cheaper, No Sightseeing, Easy Transport in Lower Ilisia]

Ilisia is also 3 km from the Acropolis hill and 3kms from Kolonaki area. Ilisia is the place where the biggest university of Greece lies, the University of Athens, which has 80.000 students.

Moreover, it is really close to the National Technical University of Athens, which has another 10.000 students. So, it is the area of Athens that is mostly inhabited by students and young people.

Ilisia is split into two areas: Upper and Lower Ilisia, or "Ano Ilisia" and "Kato Ilisia" as it is called in Greek. The Lower Ilisia is on the foot of Ilisia's hill and closer to the center of Athens and to Kolonaki area. This is where Hilton hotel lies. The Upper Ilisia are on the hill and we would not recommend staying there, as it is more difficult to walk and to get to other places. There is no underground station in Upper Ilisia.

Lower Ilisia is closer to two underground stations, the one at the Concert Hall of Athens, and the underground station of "Evangelismos" which is close to Hilton hotel.

This area is also safe but it doesn't have any monuments, important museums or other things to explore. You can find better prices than staying at Plaka or Kolonaki.

An area you should avoid to stay while you are in Athens is the area in the Omonoia square. It is probably the most dangerous area in Athens, with a lot of illegal activities, including drug dealing and prostitution and a lot of small burglary taking place.

The best hotels to stay in Ilisia are:

a. Hilton Hotel in Ilisia, Athens: Click to See Rates, Reviews and Book Online the Hilton Hotel in Athens (https://goo.gl/dnWGer)

b. Divani Caravel Hotel in Ilisia, Athens: Click to See Rates, Reviews and Book Online the Divani Caravel Hotel in Athens (https://goo.gl/aAdBVo)

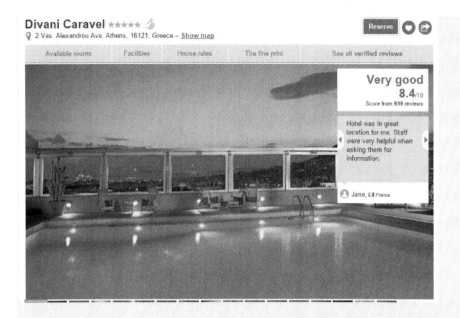

2. Staying at the North Suburbs of Athens [Posh, Safer for Families, More Expensive]

Let's have a look now at the opportunities that the North Suburbs of Athens offer for your stay. North Suburbs in general, are considered to be the areas where the upper middle class of Greeks stays at, especially in the posh areas of Kifisia, Ekali, and Dionysos. As you can imagine, the inhabitants of these areas of Athens, worry the least about the capital controls in Greece!

They don't feature museums, ancient sights or anything really touristic.

Here, you will find three many areas with hotels: Halandri, Marousi, and Kifisia.

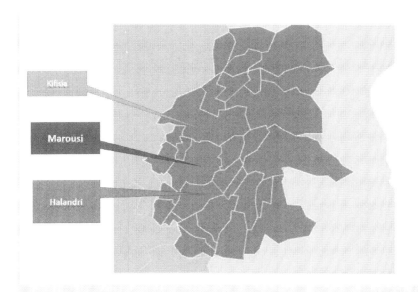

Where to Stay in Athens – Map of the North Suburbs

2a. Staying at Halandri

Halandri is a great northern suburb of Athens. It's full of restaurants, bars and is very safe. It is a very vivid place and it's much "happier" to hang around when compared e.g. to Marousi.

It has an underground station but it is not that close to the center of Halandri. If you take a taxi from here to the center of Athens, so as to visit the more touristic areas, you will have to pay around 15 to 20 euros and it is a 30-minute drive, with all the traffic of Athens.

The best hotels to stay in Chalandri (or Halandri) are:

1. The Athens Habitat Hotel: Click to See Rates, Reviews, and Book Online the Athens Habitat Hotel (https://goo.gl/CqtmKi)

Athens Habitat
Saronikou 5 & Lagadion, Athens, 15125, Greece – Show map

Available rooms | Facilities | House rules | The fine print | See all verified reviews

Superb 9.2/10
Score from 405 reviews

Large and very comfort room, excellent service, nice staff, free parking

Sergey, 30 Israel

2. The Civitel Olympic Hotel: Click to See Rates, Reviews, and Book Online the Civitel Olympic Hotel (https://goo.gl/ABmPPK)

Civitel Olympic ★★★★
Kifisias Avenue 2A & Pantanassis, Athens, 151 25, Greece – Show map

Available rooms | Facilities | House rules | The fine print | See all verified reviews

Very good
8.3/10
Score from 77 reviews

Clean and comfortable. Breakfast was amazing.

Amanda, USA

2b. Staying at Marousi

Marousi is the business center of Athens. All the big multinational companies and the biggest greek companies, such as the National Telecommunications Company, have their offices here.

Marousi is a really safe area to stay at, however, it doesn't offer too much other than that. It has a nice central square with cafes and restaurants and it has the electric train of Athens passing from its center. You will need around 40 minutes with the train to reach the center of Athens.

Marousi is around 12 km away from Acropolis. You can find cheaper hotels to stay but you will pay the price of having to move all the time with the train or a taxi towards the center of Athens.

If you choose to stay here, get a taxi and go out at Halandri or Nea Erythraia in the evening, as Marousi is quieter when it comes to nightlife.

2c. Staying at Kifissia

Semiramis Hotel in Kefalari Square at Kifisia

Kifisia is a posh area of Athens. It is on the same level (if not even higher) with Kolonaki area. Here you will find many villas from some of the richest Greeks, a great shopping center with expensive jewelry, clothes and shoes, fantastic restaurants and posh nightclubs.

Kifisia's best areas are the Kefalari Square – where you can find some nice hotels to stay at and the center of Kifisia, where its shopping center exists. Be careful not to stay at Nea Kifisia, which is a new area that is close to the national road of Athens and doesn't offer many things to do. The hotels in Kifisia are quite expensive.

If you choose to stay here, you will have only the choice of the electric train to get to the center of Athens, in around 45 minutes. There is no underground station in Kifisia. It is a really safe area to stay at.

The best hotels to stay in Kifissia are:

1. The Theoxenia Palace: Click to See Rates, Reviews, and Book Online the Theoxenia Palace (https://goo.gl/rH4efL)

2. The Semiramis Hotel: Click to See Rates, Reviews and Book Online the Semiramis Hotel in Kifissia (https://goo.gl/fAP8Zm)

Semiramis ★★★★★
📍 48 Charilaou Trikoupi Str., Kifissia, Athens, 145 62. Greece – Show map

| Available rooms | Facilities | House rules | | See all verified reviews |

Fabulous
8.6/10
Score from 188 reviews

Nice place to relax. Excellent staff service and great restaurant by the swimming pool. Lovely rooms with all extras provided

Michael, Cyprus

3. The Y Hotel in Kifissia: Click to See Rates, Reviews and Book Online the Y Hotel in Kifissia (https://goo.gl/JpjXTw)

The Y Hotel ★★★
📍 3 Myconou Str., Athens, 14562. Greece – Show map

| Available rooms | Facilities | House rules | The fine print | See all verified reviews |

Superb 9.3/10
Score from 265 reviews

Excellent hotel in an equally appealing area

Phivos, Cyprus

3. Staying at Piraeus

Piraeus is the second biggest town in the prefecture of Athens, after ..well, Athens. It is home to the famous team of "Olympiacos" and has the biggest port in Greece and one of the biggest in Europe.

Piraeus is on the beach of Athens, however, you cannot swim here, as the water is polluted. You will find many restaurants with excellent sea view (Ahinos restaurant is one of them for example) and quite a few hotels.

The good thing about staying at Piraeus is that if you are planning to get a boat to any greek island, you will be only 10 minutes away from the port. Boats to every greek island, even the best kept secret greek islands, leave from Piraeus' port.

Piraeus is not close to the center of Athens, so you will be needing at least 30 minutes to get there. It has an electric train but no underground stations. The prices of hotels are lower than the ones in the center of Athens.

One of the best areas of Piraeus is called "Kastela" and it is the hill that overlooks a nice beach area of Piraeus.

Restaurant at Kastela in Piraeus

4. Staying at the South Suburbs of Athens

Let's have a look at the South Suburbs of Athens. The South Suburbs of Athens offer you the opportunity to be next to the beaches of Athens and you will find it easy to swim at one them.

The main hotel areas are the neighborhoods of Palaio Faliro, Alimos, Elliniko, Glyfada, Voula, and Vouliagmeni.

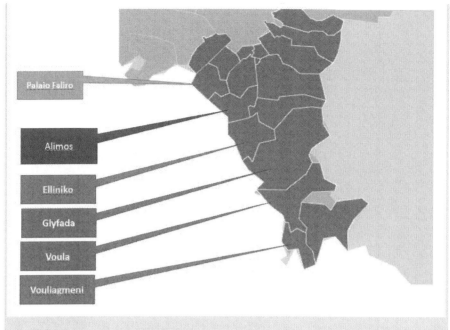

Where to Stay in Athens – Map of the South Suburbs

We will not get into much detail about each area in the Southern Suburbs of Athens. First of all, let us tell you that these are better places to stay at if you are looking into enjoying the beach, so you may not want to stay here from November to April, in the heart of the greek winter.

The most convenient time to swim at the beaches of Athens is from June to late September. Sometimes May is a nice month too or October can prove to be quite hot as well.

From all these areas, here is a quick review:
– Best Beaches: The best beach is in Vouliagmeni and is called "Asteras Vouliagmenis". It is a private beach and you will have to pay 17 euros per person from Monday to Friday and 25E per person on the weekends to swim there. Voula and Vouliagmeni have also nice beaches. Generally, the more far you go from the center of Athens, the

better the beaches get. It's not nice to swim at Palaio Faliro or Elliniko – or at least we don't like it that much.

– Best Overall Area: Glyfada is the best overall area. It has the best shopping center in the south, the best night clubs, restaurants and easy going style. It also features many hotels. The downside of Athens is that it doesn't have an underground station.

– Best Access to the Center of Athens: Elliniko, Alimos, and Palaio Faliro have the best access to the center of Athens. Elliniko and Alimos have underground stations which will get you easily to the center of Athens. If you stay at Glyfada, you will have to get to Elliniko and get the metro from there.

5. Athens Areas to Avoid

As every town in the world, Athens has some areas that you should better avoid either due to security reasons or due to difficult access to everything that the town has to offer. The areas that we suggest that you avoid is Omonoia Square in the center of Athens, the whole area close to the main train station of Athens called "Larissis Station", the Patisiwn street area and the Metaxourgeio area, even though the latter one has been upgraded during the last years and offers some gourmet restaurants.

Thank You!

Thank you for choosing this Guidora guide to Athens. We really hope that it is going to help you to make the most out of your stay in Athens.

If you have any feedback on how to improve, or if you just had a great time in Athens and you'd like to share that, just send us an email to admin@guidora.com.

Have an amazing time in Athens!

Your friends at Guidora.

Copyright Notice

Guidora Athens in 3 Days Travel Guide ©

Note to other copyright owners